Rodney died on 16 September 2014
soon after finishing this book.
He was dearly loved and is greatly missed.

Rodney at Oak Cottage, 2012

Putting It Bluntly

Outspoken Poems
by Rodney Bowsher

Acknowledgements and Thanks to:

Philip G. Keen: for cover artwork, line drawings on pp. 70 and 71 and permisssion to use photograph on p.56 (pkeen30@btinternet.com)

Ian Beech, Dan Haynes, Tim King, Timmy Naylor and Gail Parfitt: for generously contributing their poems to this book

Rosemary Barber: for commissioning 'Molly and Tom' to be read at Shobrooke Church Harvest Festival, 2014

John Katon and Tim King: for the use of the video images of Rodney on p.90 and p.101

All Saints Church, Reading: for permission to use the two photographs on p.20

Mark C. Skinner: for formatting and layout (mark@bytescomputers.co.uk)

Shirley Carew, Heather Chadwick, Frédérique Cooke, Joy Moore, Gail Parfitt, Jane Pickering and Mark C. Skinner: for editorial support

Author's Foreword

If these poems make you feel uncomfortable, change seats!
They are intended as antidotes to the everyday viruses of boredom
and ignorance. Some may have a calming effect if read aloud to
chickens, dogs, cats, goldfish, rabbits, cows, horses, monkeys,
budgies and nervy humanoids.

Be assured, this book is safe to read in armchairs, aircraft, beds,
bubble baths, buses, car parks, cruise liners, churchyards, hospitals,
public parks, prison cells, spaceships, toilets, tube trains, waiting
rooms and wheelchairs.

To help you cope with the psychological effects of these poems,
why not organise a 'mood-change' kit? If you do *not* like the book
you will need: an aspirin sandwich, a chopping board, a book to put
on the board, six eggs to put on the book, a wooden mallet to smash
the eggs, a book fixed to a plywood sign-board with a post to
support it, a long, empty field with a bank at one end to act as a
back-stop, a spotting 'scope, one hundred rounds of tracer ammo., a
7.62 general purpose machine gun, a calm, windless day, and later, a
drawing pin to put on the author's chair.

If you *do* like the book, you will need: a magnum of champagne, six
slices of toasted bread and dripping - especially the black stuff from
the bottom of the bowl with extra salt, a box of plain chocolates,
hand wipes, a copy of this book and a phone or a cheese board
tablet with a Senna pod, bipod, tripod or pea pod with which to
recommend the book to your friends.

Good luck...I'll see you inside!

Contents

Nets

Not for lobbing balls over;
Catching fish;
Practising batting;
Protecting hairdo's;
Keeping birds off:

More a subject for debate
Between two Mums
Out by the gate.

"Well, I finally got *my* new nets up,"
Said one to the other.
"Wouldn't be without 'em,"
Declared her neighbour.

The 'newly-netted' was my Mum,
Victim of war-time weakness -
Left alone to cope
With bringing up the six of us.

She sees but isn't seen
Behind the pixels of her muslin screen,
Parting, peering and closing,
Feeding a need for knowing,

Pausing to up-date herself -
"No wonder the milkman's late -
The time he spends at number eight,
Refilling that woman's crate!"

"Mum, that's embarrassing:
People can see you!"
"Son, I'm not looking out;
I'm stopping them looking in.

I'm tidying... just tidying."

Mr. and Mrs. Gibbs

(Mr. Gibbs)

He lived opposite.
Six feet tall; blood-stained apron;
White trilby; black wellies:
He could have been a porter,
Filleting fish.

Instead of which,
He shouldered carcasses of pork
On and off a lorry
For the Danish Bacon Company.

A former Sergeant Major,
His shout could be heard
Three fields away,
Where I played with his son.

We didn't need watches:
At precisely four, came the roar
Which lasted all of twenty seconds:
'Myi, iy, iy CAAALL!'
Michael felt ashamed and sad;
"*Got* to go...that was my Dad!"

After tea, touching to see
Such a tower of power
Raking the ground,
Round his prize cauliflower.

(Mrs. Gibbs)

Mrs. G was slender,
With natural curly hair;
Sensible but tender:
My mother's favourite neighbour.

On Wednesdays at three,
Mum and me
Went over for tea
To Mrs. Gibbs' parlour.

I had the arm-chair by the fire
Close to the chiming clock.
Boing! Boing!
Tick-tock.

Meanwhile, the Mums tuned in
To the BBC.
And 'Mrs. Dale's Diary.'

I sat with comics:
Pictures and bubbles
Of heroic troubles...
"Sergeant Steel!"
"Lootenant?"
"We gotta clear the Krauts
Off that goddamned hill!"

Every Wednesday,
That's where we'd be:
The Magnificent Seven
In our bit of heaven:
Two Mums,
A wireless,
A ticking clock,
A lump of cake,
A cup of tea
And me.

Never before or since,
Have I felt so safe;
Been so happy;
Or known such peace.

Tick-tock tick-tick...

Big Boy

Three bored boys,
Playing in a quarry, empty on a Saturday:
Two of them brothers - easy to see -
One twelve and one ten, same as me.

"Who's got the biggest Willy?" says big boy.
"Get 'em out so we can see."
His Willy test was silly,
So little was there in it, really!

Big boy would *not* let go.
"I know! Let's see who can pee the highest.
You two with maggots shouldn't worry,
You can still have fun, even with a little one...

Scratch your names
In that sandy bank.
The game is to aim at your name."

Things were out of order:
They had swigs of water.
I wanted to go home.

It was a farce.
In both events
I came last.

'A Man is Being Held '

'He felt himself to be a nobody;
He had low self-esteem,'
Goes the familiar theme.

" 'E kept 'imself to 'imself,
Very quiet, but 'e seemed nice."
Quotes a neighbour,
In front of the lights.

So why don't the rest of us give it a go?
It could be fun...
Being on the telly
With close-ups of our gun.

Designer Fatigue

I worked in *Coats* at a menswear store.
They sent me to a factory near Glastonbury Tor,
Makers of hides our clients wore.

Our tour began on the factory floor.
"Tanning and quality are the key.
When we tan your hides
You get the best thirty-three!"

Next, a meeting of the Board:
"Any questions?" asked the Chair.
"Yes, young man, you down there."

"Chair, your quality-controller says
The skins you send are the best...
But if the cows from which they came
Have been scratching their arses
On barbed-wire fences,
Why should we pay the same?"

"Good question: the answer is, young man,
For no extra fee you'd be getting free
The latest skins in *'Designer Fatigue*!'
Your order will be whatever you want.
Now we must adjourn to the restaurant."

On the way, he humoured me.
"Is there something you'd like?
Gloves? Ours would be a luxury,
Made from Cape Napa,
The world's finest leather."

"Now you mention it,
My frisky girl-friend Freda -
She prefers Fred - has often said how she
Would *love* a leather spread to cover our bed,
Perhaps in Cape Napa?"

"Sorry, sir, not a job we'd undertake.
Too expensive:
Would take two years to make.
Mmm, that smells good; I think it's steak!"

That night, I popped out to see the sights:
A few closed shops,
A reflection in a window of myself,
Between the shadows of the Cathedral
And a half-lit launderette.
The only other light, the yellow orbs
Of the zebra crossing, teasing the road
With their on and offing.

With the sun's setting,
The Tor was gone from sight,
Blackened by the ink of night -
But not the field, back-lit by the street
Where fifty dozing steam-irons
Puffed vapours into air
And hunkered down in circles,
Away from barbs on fences,
Strung out everywhere.

Watching their lashes flicking off rain
I felt guilt and shame, seeing
Not fifty cows, but fifty factories...
About to become belts, wallets, gum,
Purses, shoes, hand-bags, arm-chairs,
Cases, car seats, jackets, watch-straps;
House of Commons benches and COATS!
Not forgetting their begetting of milk,
Stock-cubes, beef-dripping and STEAKS!

Such big, sad eyes: I couldn't cope.
I hurried back for a large, stiff drink!
As to what I'd felt?
Best not to mention it.

Purrchance to Dream

Dirty feet and paddy paws,
Openmouth, lickity pinkity jaws,
Snuggily snubbily nosing in fluffery,
Back from your streetleaping birdbashing toughery.
One eye asleep and awake in the other,
Asthmatic mother and dog-killed brother,
Caramel gingerish pinkish and cream,
Wolsey cat Wolsey cat where have you been?
Lying there curled up furled up and fat,
What do cats dream about:

… Crème de la Sprat?

At the Zoo

If the reverse were true
And animals studied humans,
What do you suppose
They would make of you?

Inverse Law

Bounce a ball against a wall:
The angle of return
Reflects the angle of approach.

Likewise, I'm vain and selfish,
Thinking only of myself.
Why...?
Because nobody else is.

Maggots

I don't mind
If I eat fish
Which eat maggots
I fish with.
Maggots eat me
When my fishing days
Are finished with.

Singing in the Choir

At 'All Saints', Reading,
There was always a schism
Between me and religion.
Five bob for weddings;
Five bob for funerals;
An outing to the seaside once a year.
My business with holy ground...?
It paid more than a paper round!

Unlike the 'confirmed,'
I did *not* grope Guides and Brownies;
Strip lead from the roof;
But *did* repeat the vicar's bits -
The last one, his best:
'The peace of mind
Which passeth all understanding,
Shall keep your hearts and minds
At rest.'

Our thoughts switched from Godly good
To roast beef and Yorkshire pud.
Flippers together, we prayed and sang,
Mumbling our way through with aching bums,
From a hard pew in that cold, damp, pointy place.
Feeling less spiritual than physical:
Finding it hard to stand with pins and needles
And leave with a serious face.

I still try, every New Year's Eve,
To look up at the sky and feel *something*!
Ugh! Ugh! Ugh!
But...NOTHING!
Only the warmth from a sherry
And a hot sausage roll
In a cold, old hand.

S.SMITH. G.BOWERS. J.CARBOUGER. J.RADDS. G.SAFFENDEN. P.WHITE. R.WILLIAMS. A.LANG. B.PAYES. R.TAYLOR. A.BERRY. W.JOHNSON. R.MAYNE.
/SACRISTAN/
C.PEPWORTH. G.GRANT. B.PRICE. R.N.GREEN. REV.L.R.SIDLEY M.A. R.N.NASS. S.THOMAS. E.GILES. M.MAYNE. I.SMITH.
/SECRETARY/ /PRIEST-IN-CHARGE/ /ORGANIST/
J.RAWLING. P.ATKINSON. M.LINGWELL. J.SCOTT. A.BAGGE. A.SNOW. N.HARDCASTLE. J.FRAZER. L.WALKER. R.HUTCHINSON. J.WOODWARD. R.BUCKNELL. E.BOWDEN.

Handyman

If you can cope with the simple knack
Of winding a plug round a wash-basin tap,
It shows your brain can be led
To favour function over fashion,
Improving instead, on what was in the box
With what is in your head.

After years of inventing and D.I.Y.ing,
If you were dying in the night,
Would it seem right
For those who rifled your patch
To scrap or steal your cache?   No.

But you *can* take it with you when you go.
So when your world turns black,
Let events speak for themselves
And the last word be yours
On how to get your patents back...

Attach them to a booby trap.

Big Strong Man

I woke from a dream
Full of wrath
And saw
On the wall above my head,
A giant moth.

I squashed it flat
With a hard-back book,
But it wouldn't die...

It was a picture hook!

Tea with the Colonel in Lymington, Hants.
(1970's)

Bridge and backgammon are the games played here,
By widowed Colonels and retired Rear-Admirals,
Searching for their slippers and Fortnum's kippers,
Admitting married daughters have 'their own lives' now.

Which is why I've been so quiet, Sir,
Whilst you have been so loud.

For whatever I am rooted in, be sure it's not this…
Though visiting me would leave you likewise disappointed
Since I very seldom drink, or use a T.V. set's enticements
To take me where I'm not, and all the 'Five-Star' in the World
Won't warm from me a "Bravo!" or a "Frightfully well-ridden!"
For some bouncing Jack or Jill, clipping four seconds off
In the show-jumping at Hickstead.

Which is why I've been so quiet, Sir,
Whilst you have been so loud.

But - to answer the question which your gimlet eye demands -
Yes, I have 'done that' with the girl who dragged me here
To meet her mother's '*old friend*'.
The girl whose arse you've just been patting;
Whose plate you're overloading.
A wife…a daughter substitute? That's not my care…
It's just your dogged bloody-mindedness
Which won't admit to loneliness, for fear of *the shame,*
Which I can't bear.

Which is why I've been so quiet, Sir,
Whilst you have been so loud…

Food Chain

I died and rotted into earth.
Maggots got to work.
One, in particular, enjoyed my brain
And stuffed himself silly
Until a worm arrived
And to the maggot did the same.

It rained.
The worm surfaced.
A passing blackbird saw its chance
And - thanks to this bonus of the cemetery -
Swooped down and slurped it up.

Later, when the bird fed its chicks,
I got the bits
Of brain, maggot and worm
Which gave me strength to depart the nest
For a tree next to a supermarket car-park.

Once a week, my widow parked there,
In the space *we* always used.
She enjoyed watching the birds.
One - in particular - perched closely above,
Amused her with its antics,
Hopping up and down
In a manner most peculiar.

She watched and she wept.
I cried out but she couldn't see
That the bird she was watching . . .
Was me.

Blood

When blood is warm,
Creatures of all species
Are duly born.

When blood boils,
Triggers are pulled
And flesh is torn.

When blood is cold,
Time is up
For the old.

Whatever its role -
Whatever it triggers...

The rich man's laugh;
The poor man's toil;

Always in the arteries,
Hot or cold -
Blood performs its role.

'Part Ones'

Whereas kids just want to play,
Those of us now wobbling
Like to organize our day.
At 8am we're found in dressing gowns,
Motionless, with vacant stare,
Caught between thoughts, going nowhere,
Only the sorting office of the mind
Where we parcel up the day
Into the minutiae of what to do, where to go,
Who to phone and what to say.

A tick list of the most to least urgent
Is a good idea:
Even in the Army, at 8am
We would appear around a notice board,
To learn from 'Part One Orders'
Where to be, at what time,
In what mode of dress and for what purpose.
Doubtless, our survivors will also have a list,
Called the 'Order of Service' telling them
What they need to know
On the day they watch us go.

Marriage Vows

Two slices of bread.
She has a slice,
He has a slice.
She cuts hers in half,
And gives half to him.
He cuts his in half,
And gives half to her.
So... what do they become,
Half of what they were?

Door

There is no reprieve from death except life.
No reprieve from life except death,
No 'Use by' date.
It starts with a cry
And ends with a vapour of breath,
Evaporating up,
Before the door below the bottom step
Is shut.

Case for the Defence

A little bit of sun peeped out today
And bounced about the traffic
In Ealing Broadway.
It bounced off Woolworth's
And Associated Pumps
And I bounced into
The car in front.

Collision

Lest we forget,
It's not a bird's fault
When it flies into a jet.

Nor is it right
To call a plane strike
A bird strike.

So fuck the loss
From the shareholder's purse!
Who do you suppose was up there first?

Flypast

The Royals waved
To the crowds below,
Giving the jets
A token glance.

A Republican pigeon,
Seizing its chance,
Took careful aim
And crapped...

Everybody clapped!

Heaven's Bird

Inevitably, determinedly,
The woodpecker chips away at our tree,
Ignoring leaves, twigs and branches
For the trunks of you and me.

Seconds, minutes, hours, days, weeks,
Months and years are pecked away,
Until nothing can be found:
Just a patch of sawdust,
Fading into ground.

Molly and Tom

Molly and Tom were from Crediton.
They met when he put the chain back on
Her Rudge-Whitworth bike.
She was sixteen; he was seventeen;
It was nineteen fifteen.
They talked as he worked
On the grass by the park.
Smitten...he took his time with the task.

She wore a high-necked blouse
With leg-of-mutton sleeves,
A cameo brooch at her throat;
She had glossy black hair,
Tucked under a wide-brimmed hat
Trimmed with lace,
Which she kindly took off
To fan his face.

He was six foot tall, hands like shovels,
Waistcoat and cap,
Struggling to hold his blond curls back.

When jobs would allow,
They met for a year.
Molly worked at the Manor,
Tom followed the plough.
As the news got worse, they stayed close,
Struggling to put head before heart,
Before the War pulled them apart.

In 1916, aged eighteen,
Along with other volunteers,
Tom was sent for by the Devonshires;
Destination: France...
A place of slender chance.

No more larking about
On sunny, birdsong days,
Mixing work and play
On a trailer-load of hay.

Gone forever, their hands on a gate,
A cow's udders, a sheep's fleece.
Gone too, the social rub: the click and shove
Of dominoes, pies and pints at the village pub.
No more throwing a 'double-top';
Cueing the billiards for an 'in off.'
Guns no longer for rabbiting
But for other mothers' sons:
Like them, denied growing old
By doing what they were told.
Small comfort for mothers
If they died to save others.

Going 'over the top',
The Sergeant's parting shot:
"Remember lads, it's either them or us!"
So it was, but not for those
Who started the fuss...
Covering their tracks
With poppies and plaques.

Wars..?
Ask not who's going to die,
Who's going to cry
But who starts them
And why?

Hereafter,
Let us harvest only corn -
Never again, the corpses
Of men and horses.

Hearts and Minds
(Dedicated to Anna and John)

They loved each other
But one lived and one died.
The one who survived
Returned to the place
Where love thrived:
The town of St. Ives.

A place of soft breezes
Brushing the face,
Of secret spots
And fond embrace,
A place where they
Walked the sands,

Arm in arm,
Hand in hand.
One is living
And one has died,
But not in the heart,
Or in the mind.

Little Box of Chocs

Death is a box of chocs
With mainly two to choose from:
Burial or cremation.

The first could be worse:
Its legacy, just dirt
Or re-birth as an insect,
Rodent, reptile, bird, rabbit,
Grass, weed, flower, bush or tree.

The second is harder to see:
It could be that bone, ashes,
Grit and potassium bits
Help the drainage and fertility
Of the first.

Or maybe – if you opt for a public place –
Keen devotees of cemeteries
Will walk all over you,
While a man with a parish stipend
Bends over a mower
For his monthly make-over
Of the beds of the dead.

Who's to say?
Maybe we leave the ground anyway
And just hang in the air, as clouds,
Waiting to come down again –
As life-giving rain.

Side Room 4
(August 2014)

Small, with a heavy fire door,
To keep me in
And others out.
One small window
Which doesn't open
And looks out upon
A white, brick wall.
Altogether a concrete womb:
An isolation room.

Before Nothing

When it's time to go,
May it be in a state of grace,
Looking up at a loved one's face,

Not vacantly staring -
Without registering -
At a hospital ceiling

Showing signs of neglect
And peeling
With emulsified tears.

Putting It Bluntly

The doctor told me, as best he could,
"Things are not looking good".

I dwelt on it in bed,
And saw myself, instead,
Out in the open,
Teetering along the top
Of a ten foot high,
Six-inch thick brick wall.

On the left,
A green sweet-smelling meadow,
On the right, a burnt-out field,
Blackened and charred.

Day and night, the wind blows,
Always from left to right.
It's getting stronger.

Unless it drops,
I cannot stay on top
Much longer.

Death of a Para

He lived alone,
With faded photos around his home:
Reminders of kidding
With mates in the rigging.

His breathing now shallow,
He reached beneath the pillow;
Placed his beret on his chest,
And declared a valediction
To what he recalled best.

He imagined he could see -
Above the exit - a twin glow...
His last words mimicking
An RAF dispatcher:

'Stand up!'
'Hook up!'
'Stand in the door!'
'Red light!'
'Green light!'...

'GO!'

Two Chump Chops

You said it was me, I said it was you.
In truth, it was both of us,
Getting the bus to the County Court.
Inside, we found a wire grill
On which a sign was hung,
Marking the end of coupledom:

A corrugated lid from a cardboard box,
Lop-sided on a swing of frayed string.
DIVORCES it said, in felt-tip red.
Behind the glass, a face appeared.
"Sir; Madam; sign here - and here."
One fee, one decree and one minute later,
Our marriage was dead.

Outside - a terminus:
We got the same seats on the same bus.
Our fares? What a wheeze!
"Two *singles* please."
The bus stopped. Alone, I got off.

At home, on their own at the back of the fridge,
Two chump chops, on the bone.
Why did she leave *two* ?
Confused, I wondered what to do:
Cook one of them...or two!?

Litterbug

In the wastepaper basket
At the bottom of her heart
Lies me
Lies you,
And God knows how many
Before she's through
With disposing of her litter,
The litter of the bitter.

A Ripping Yarn

Since the worth of places seen
And events pursued
Is far less dependent
On where than with whom,

What then is there left to see
And what can I pursue,
Knowing places and events
So depended on you?

And how can I evade the past
And go beyond its boundary,
If every time I climb a fence
My heart snags on a memory?

Swingtime

Watching golfers at the Driving Range
Shows brute force doesn't mean power,
Any more than politeness means weakness
And proves the means, not the end,
Is the golfer's truest friend.

Watch the men:
Five buckets of balls from some of them
And five buckets of expletives!
Before frowning at the club-heads after mis-hits.

Watch the women:
One bucket of balls in the time of five;
Rhythmical, poised, swinging within limits -
To a smooth follow-through and a high, balanced finish.

After a lesson, the men can't go
Without mumbling rhetorical alibis
To a sky-gazing Pro'.

Whereas women - after playing -
Listen politely, book their next lesson
Then go...
Back to the business of living.

Androgyny

Gimme a woman who smokes, swears and spits,
Not some laser-voiced clothes peg
Opining about fish.
Some Sue or Prue, with nothing to do,
Except *organize* !
Gimme a woman who can use her fists,
Fix a car and whistle a riff.

Gimme a woman with bee-sting lips,
A fat-free Amazon with muscular tits.
A gravelly-voiced skinhead, a manly Miss:
Happy to squat all day in a ditch,
One hand on her shotgun,
The other on my zip.
Gimme a woman who smokes, swears and spits.

Monday . . . The Nine to Five Coronaries
(1970's)

Here they come, in sensible brogues,
Champions of the eight o'clock dash,
Making the change from Sunday to Monday,
From egg-stained yawn to cigarette ash.

It's an ugly-people train,
The step-down train
To Piccadilly Circus
From Rayner's Lane.

A terrifying peep-show
Of got-up got-at faces,
An exposé of tired fat
In Christmas present braces.

Crouching over crosswords
They pigeonhole their worth.
I can't believe the clues they seek
Are up that au pair's skirt.

Count the Parkers in their pockets,
Spot the shirts of yellowing white,
Note the make-up on a shoulder
Left by someone else's wife.

Sitting like a six-pack of take-away men,
Were they ever like me
And will I be like them?
The nine to five coronaries confront me again.

Top Eye

With the flutter
Of each elliptical shutter
Struggling not to wake up
And the bottom eye
Deep in the pillow,

What the top eye sees
On the bedside table,
Shows we don't amount to much:

A spiteful clock,
A puddle of change,
More copper than silver,
A bunch of keys,
In random order

And when it's humid,
A storm-fly,
Flapping on top
Of a glass of water.

Fizzing and Sparking

When the body craves sleep
But the mind denies it,
Because they both refuse to fit,
Fizzing and sparking
Like an arc-welding kit:
What about posture?

Flat on your back,
Feet together?
Legs scissored apart?
Try the left side?
The right side?
Lie face-down?
Make yourself
A question mark?

Count sheep?
Vestal virgins?
Be ready to go
After cock crow?
Will the dawn chorus
Render you oblivious?
NO,NO,NO!

Hours later
And it's *still* 5am.
To knit mind and body
The only strategy:
Dip them both together
Into a big mug of tea.

Hide and Seek

Children chant and play a game
In which they run and hide.
Adults play it too -
Hiding what's inside.

Are they both the same?
Children say what they mean,
Adults put up a screen,
Afraid to take a dare.

'Come out! Come out!
Whoever you are;
We *know* you're there!'

Lifeline

Draw a line
Down the middle
Of your mind.

Nothing in front,
Nothing behind,
Nothing better
Than the other.

Our mistake,
Life's oldest:
Too much pencil,
Not enough rubber.

Natural Wastage

(I)

Christine Oates had sixteen coats
Hung on a silver rail.
She loved to shop
But not to stop
To pay the bill as well.
Will she survive a coat-free cell?
Only time will tell.

(II)

Valerie Garrity managed a charity
Taking in millions of pounds.
Losses occurred and Val was transferred
To the prison at Holloway.
There, she helps crooks find suitable books
On cases of Corporate Bribery.

(III)

Norman Norris loved his job,
In a 'high end' cycle shop,
A treasure trove of sparkling chrome,
A job he'd never swap.
Norman loved the rows of 'bling' -
They made him feel at home.
'Buy a Bike from Dingaling!'
It said above the phone.

Norman wrote orders for punters;
Some, he wrote for himself.
He left with lumps in his trousers,
The size of the gaps on the shelf.
He wasn't much worried by cables,
Nor gears or saddles or chain,
As much as the practical problems
Of wearing the wheels and the frame.

The answer was plain:
Return what he took,
Finish his project and hide it.
Then using his key after work,
Sneak out the bike and ride it.
Christmas had come early:
The currants were in the bun.
The system had provided
A Rolls-Royce for his bum.
Job done, my son, job done!

(IV)

Tom and Sonia Farmer
Worked for Huntley and Palmer,
Biscuit manufacturer.
Their main responsibility,
The handling of security.
Every night they manned the gates
And searched for hidden bics and cakes.

Tom discovered doughnut rings
Behind men's hanging things.
Sonia spotted ginger-nuts
Tucked into brassiere cups.

Known as the 'deadly duo,'
They groped their way to the top.
Their one big disappointment?
They weren't allowed to swap.

It would've led to better stats
On catching-rates and rhythm:
Sonia could've groped the men
And Tom could do the women.

With factory gone and both retired,
Their searching days are over.
No one's left for them to search,
Except for one another.

She checks him for betting slips;
He checks her for cigarettes;
She checks teeth aren't left in bed:
He checks that the dog is fed.

All is in its dotage,
Workers and buildings alike,
Victims of 'natural wastage',
The shoplifter of life.

Crediton

Devon: a grassy egg-box county, in the midst of which
In its green cavity, lies the priceless egg of Crediton:
Older than a Fabergé, yet fresh as the birth
Of its founder, Saint Boniface, in 680 AD.

It can still surprise by what it provides,
Being neither too large nor too small,
A comfy size, like a favourite jacket
Wrapping its arms around houses and farms.

A place not just for buying and selling,
But narrowing the pavement to socialise.
Afterwards, sharing the re-play...
"Guess who I saw in town today!?"

A place worth stopping for,
Where fun and function touch each generation,
Passing the baton from old to young
In our proud town of Crediton.

Statues

They are found the world over,
In parks and town centres.
Marbled perennials, history's sentinels
Guarding the flower-beds.

Some were leaders, inventors, explorers,
Hardly likely to live next door to us;
Kings, generals, adventurers,
Sent to loot countries defended by spears.

Their legacy now,
To sit astride chargers,
Raising a sabre; a lanyarded Webley;
Shielding their eyes from the dust of an enemy.

New threats are met:
Graffiti, jets, the rush-hour's drone,
A hat undermined by a traffic cone,
Left for a lark by a lagered-up loon.

Birds nest in the horse's mouth,
Eyeing the ground
For daily treats, shared out
By lunch-time crowds.

Words on the plinth are indistinct,
Chipped and blurred, like horse and rider;
Both reined back by time and weather
From making their final charge.

Their moment in history over,
Their fame temporary.
In such ways, selectively,
Do we punctuate the past.

From the dock of his floral plot,
It's the statue whose verdict will stick:
'Once we were covered in glory...
Now we are covered in shit!'

Budleigh Salterton

A coastal path
Meanders above.
Be careful if it's muddy:
You could end up in Budleigh.

Know that women of Budleigh Salterton
Never put shorts and halters on.
Age dictates instead,
They perch along the prom
Keeping rain off heads
Beneath waterproof condoms
While chatting to a neighbour
About offspring in Australia.

There are many shops
Without parking spots.
A quirky place, where scissors cost
As much as twenty pounds:
A clue to its numbers of 'comfortably off'?

Rows of painted huts -
The Council owns the lease -
Guarantee accountants
A profitable feast.
They make a festive backdrop
Strung along the beach,
Adding to the palette of red cliffs,
Sand, sea, mackerel skies
And blue-rinsed mermaids,
Zimmering by.

The place is a living post card.
But for all its watery sun
And arthritic fun,
I, for one, won't come again.
So, goodbye...
Budleigh Bloody Salterton!

Seaside B&B

Landlady says...

"Good morning, Sir, Madam!
Grapefruit segments or cereal?
Full English?
Croissant or toast?
Newspaper?
Tea or coffee?
What will it be today?"

Wife thinks...

He's not very good
In the morning.
Please, don't let him say
What I know he's thinking!

Husband thinks...

Shut you gob!
Leave us alone
And go away!

Speech Therapy

I met you briefly,
Drawn less to salient female bits
Than face and lips
Shaping bubble-light words.

Mouth, so *mobile,* so *supple,*
Portent of a perfect kiss?
Voice, graphite-smooth,
The coating on a slipway groove.
Everything you said,
A pillow for my head.

Personal baggage may damage
What separate lives can manage,
Should we ever meet again
Beyond this minute spent outside the fence.

Romantically, my record is not good,
Never daring, as I should,
To ask if doors are open or ajar.
Shut out by what I've got:
A mud pie of morality,
Legalised duality,
Barring the way
To a physical knot.

Narcissus pseudonarcissus

I knew him best when passions peaked and blood began to rise;
When hormones grew between the years, eighteen and twenty five.

Tall, slim, androgynously handsome.

No mirror managed, in or out of clothes,
To echo such perfection, from head to tips of toes.

I fought off many rivals to ensure our love's survival.

Obsessed, I followed slavishly - flattering, fawning, guarding.
Yet he was the jailer who turned the key, caging my heart indefinitely.

In mirror and mind, he became me and me became he, joined umbilically.

Now spindly, aged and flawed, the lover I saw,
I no longer recognise at my door:

I don't love him, me, him, me, him... anymore.

Launch Site

Memory revisits a rocket site.
A trellis of light, where blood excited a lift-off.
Where a polished, pink nose-cone throbbed
In the wait for 'ignition' from its pubic hob.

Women were in awe;
Panting to draw on the power of its payload.
They no longer visit the count-downs;
The launch-sight long since abandoned -

Its rocket reduced to a rubber rivet
In a dried-up gulley,
Lost beneath the overhang of time and belly.
A fading memory, a maggoty metaphor.

Who cares what it's for?
I don't... anymore.

God and Chips

God, let my horses win;
Let my ship come in;
My God; Thank you God;
God help us; Good God;

Please God, send us warmth;
Dear God, send us rain;
I promise, God: I won't do it again!

For centuries, zillions of people,
In God's name - praying, pleading,
Begging, pestering:
Driving him INSANE!

A *disgrace*!
No wonder he refuses
To show his face.

God's House?

Not wishing to intrude,
I asked where God sat.
Nobody knew.

"That's up to him..."
Said a grumpy old chap,
"But this is *my* pew!"

Cuddly Toy

Is God a toy kept on a shelf?
A substitute for someone else?
And when you take him down to play
What will you have to say?
'Make my sadness go away;
Give me joy that I can grasp,
Not slippery soap, lost in the bath.'

What if you stop and ask a shop
For a bumper bag of joy?
Their reply, like as not...

'Sorry, mate; we're out of stock.
Can do you a singing bird;
A nose job;
A nuclear watch;
A friendly dog;
A cuddly God?'

Two Chocolate Teapots

Capitalism...Communism:
They are the same,
Both denying their synergy:
Equal opportunities for everyone...
After me.

Wishful Thinking

Fawning over baby:
'Coochie, coochie, coo!'

If baby smiles,
Is it because it's you

Or would anyone do
Who could make a silly face?

Unturned Key

Are you like me?
A car nobody starts.
Not comforted, cared for, wanted,
Needed, touched or talked to?

Did you hear a teacher say,
'The team is picked:
You lot watch,
Or run around the pitch.
Find *something* to do!'
Are you like me?
Did it happen to you?

What was said in *your* report?
'He makes little cakes and pastries.'
'She's good at climbing ropes?'
Were you like me, missing
A partner for the dancing?

Loneliness:
The clues lie sometimes with one's self.
To get you off the shelf,
Find a useful glue, especially if you're
Seen as too good to be true.

Getting old?
Still doing what you're told?
Have a go at 'give and take.'
Love often happens very late
So, have faith:
Wait; wait; wait!

Ballad of Sir Hadenough

Sir Hadenough was made a knight
Because he saved King Arthur's life.
His fellow knights were vain and cruel,
Rich in livestock, land and jewels.
Minstrels made them legendary,
Leaving out their acts of cruelty.

So much inconsistency
Was added to their litany:
Slaying Dragons? Yes.
Rape and Pillage? No.
Sacking of Monasteries? No.
Sir Hadenough had had enough:
A very fed-up knight!
Sick of all this *gallantry*,
This status-seeking shite.

Enough of chewing last month's deer;
Burnt old scraps of peasant's ear -
Curses on this draughty castle
And King Arthur's silly table,
Rimmed around with drunken knights,
Teasing dogs with bits of tripe.

Tired of his heavy sword,
Ex-cali-bloody-bur
And the rust along his lance,
The daftest kit of all:
He hadn't slain a dragon
Since he hung it on the wall.
Likewise, his shield,
With its vulgar, painted cover:
Three sausage dogs with lions' beards,
On top of one another.

Jaded from jousting, he went to bed
To ease the lump upon his head -
A crafty strike by the sly Black Knight.
Merlin applied a tincture of stinkture
With maggot mash, to heal the bump
And the armour rash.

Soon, our knight rejoined the fight,
Competing in the lists,
Which often left him on his arse,
Amongst the hacked-off body parts,
Which tripped the jousters up
Until the pigs came on to sup.

As champion, he waived the chance
To lower his lance to the gormless Guinevere,
Choosing instead, her neighbour, Grace,
Bladder of ale around her waist,
Pet monkey on her knee,
Hoping for a taste..

At sunset, Sir 'H' laid his head
On the flea-ridden fur
Of his straw-covered bed,
Musing on bliss with his chosen Miss
As she roasted a pig and fed him bits,
Each licking grease from the other's lips.

A crow morphed into the inky night,
Lifting from its look-out spot
And the moon threw grappling-hooks of light
Over the walls of Camelot.

a nessuna cosa
(fading to nothing)

Tired from the concert,
He took everything off:
Trousers, waistcoat, pocket-watch.
He shed the lot.

He longed for his bed
But circled instead
Around and around it,
Waving his baton
With only his hat on.

Poor old Prokofiev,
Could *not* get his socky off.
Patience gone,
He fell into bed:
One sock on,
One sock off.

State of No. 1 Bed

Friction grew
Between beds one and two
At St. Thomas's, Waterloo.

"Nurse! Nurse!
Look a' the state of No.1 bed;
Look a' the state of it!"

Little shit!
From my bed, opposite,
I saw him fix
His 'Nil by Mouth' sign
Onto his neighbour's bed;
So he would get his breakfast
And the chump would
Get the surgeon, instead!

Unhappy No. 2;
A London cabbie,
With not much left
On his clock.

"Nurse! Nurse!
'E's done it again...
Look a' the state'a
No.1 bed!"

Severance Day

Weather didn't matter,
In heat or frost, she never took it off.
In or out of water, it was what he bought her
So she never took it off.

Then she slipped on wet grass,
Her hand taking the weight:
A snap and a twist left her gasping,
Grasping a wrist no longer straight,
Broken in two places.
The emblem on a swelling finger
Would just have to come off,
So in it went, between cutter and block.

Back home she never cried,
The pain was in the heart,
Not in the wrist within the sling.
She quietly asked for a little bag
To protect something valuable she said she had,
Then quickly passed it over: a little wounded thing,
The interrupted halo of a severed wedding ring.

Wife No.5

Dust spreads in their wake:
A Bedouin Sheik leads his string
Of camels and wives
Across Saharan waste.
No palms or features show:
He knows *exactly* where to go.

Scarf around her face,
Wife No.5 rides at the back,
Choking on dust raised by rivals in front.
Her beauty threatens them.

Long lashes help her camel see
As it lopes along, sedately,
Enabling her to read her poetry,
Propped up against the pommel.
She reads aloud -
To make her camel tranquil.

When they camp at the oasis,
She hopes - Allah willing -
For a summons to her master's tent
To recite some more,
Emerging in the morning,
As wife No.4?

Yeah, Baby, Yeah…

Acoustic waves, surfed by a younger age –
Pop and prattle crashes onto the shore
Washing away what went before.
'Yeah, baby, yeah… that's what l said, l said yeah!'
It sounds - when they sing -
Like someone sat on a drawing pin.

Classical; jazz; easy listening;
Catchy tunes with legible words
Ebb away – no longer heard.
Replaced instead by the easy to sing,
Easy to play and easy to say:

'Hey, Babe… Hey!'

You Know…

Such a bore,
When people keep saying,
'You know…you know…you know…'
Because if we know –
What are they telling us for?

Waiting Factory

When days are predetermined
By a sameness of routine,
Rituals defend us
From the random and extreme.

When patients chat about their care
And skirt around their darkest fear,
A daily ritual calms them.

Not much interrupts
The rhythms of their day:
Stops for jabs and tabs;
The big deal of a meal
With its dribble, drop and spill;
The heated exchange
When a missing condiment
Becomes a major incident.

Hard on its heels,
The starchy sound
Of 'high-ups' coming round:
'And how are we today?'

'He said to me... I said to him'...
Some were glad
To be going home -
With its creature comforts.
Others sad, their way out stopped,
Leaving them stuck,
With rituals,
Like old ink blots.

What to do, between rituals?
Turn on your side; cover your face;
Block out sound; hide from light;
Wait for them to get dinner on;
Grab a moment's oblivion?

Epidemic

Doctors recognised a pattern:
A contagion of the social services.
Teachers, policemen, nurses,
The armed forces -
Even doctors had it.

It presented as stress, confusion,
A pain in the ear,
As if a foreign object was there.
Pencil lights confirmed it:
An ear with paper in it.

Their diagnosis?
A political *initiative*.

'Bumps-a-Daisy!'

Roll up, roll up…
All the fun of the fair!
Acknowledge - if you dare -
We are no more than bumping cars
Crashing, sparking, morphing
Into each other and the elements.

As mere humans,
We have less provenance, integrity,
Purpose and longevity than a rock.
Birth, childhood, relationships, marriages, families,
Homes, villages, towns, counties,
Cities, countries, the World…

Mere matter in a vast collidron;
An evolutionary pattern, made up
Not of the glue of me and you,
Passing the baton,
But a force within and beyond the Universe…
The atom.

Bereavement

There is nothing more painful
Or abrupt,
Than when the string of love
Is cut.

Love's Touch
(3 September 2014)

After forty days in a coma
I felt ten fingers soothing
My spine ...
Five were my wife's,
Five were mine.

This White House
(7 May 2004)

With fields below
And birdsong above,
This white house
Is the right house
To house our love.

This house will survive
And not permit
Fatigue, pain or worry
To sully it.

Its gardens will be scented
With calm and peace:
This white house
Is the right house
To forever please.

OAK COTTAGE 2008
DEVON   R.B.

The Herd Who Never Heard

At half-past eight the cows would wait
By the farmer's gate for their morning feed.
I'd cross the road with my clarinet
And give them a serenade.

I played:
'The Farmer and the Cowman should be Friends',
'Oh, What a Beautiful Morning', 'Summertime',
'Rhapsody in Blue'... Not even a moo!

Eyes glazed, they dribbled and muzzled the ground,
Bored by the squeaky sound.
Perhaps such a herd would have preferred
A bassoon, with its deeper voice.

When I last saw them, I told them straight:
"Next time we meet, you'll be on a plate!"
To feed them music was *such* a mistake:
I no longer play to them over the gate.

Audit

Before you go,
Up there or down below,
There are those who'd like to know
Just what you've done:
Has your snail
Left a trail?

'Well...
I've done this;
I've done that;
I've been here;
I've been there;
I've known him;
I've known her.'

But...
Have you sat under a tree?
Seen leaves fidget in the breeze?
Paddled in the sea?
Smelt a flower?
Stroked a creature?
Felt rain and sun?
Known joy and fun?
Shared sweet, fresh air?
Gazed at a starry night?
You HAVE!

Then you've done all right!

The Roundsmen
(1940's-1950's)

By various means, they made themselves known.
They shouted, rang bells and used a megaphone,
Right outside your home, so you'd know what they plied.
"Any old iron?" "Old rags for goldfish?" they cried.

A Breton Frenchman in smock and beret pushed his bike along,
100 kilos of onions draping the wheels, singing in pidgin English
His 'Johnny Onion' song:
"Shonny Oignon... Shonny Oignon!"

Also on a bike, tray on head, the Muffin Man,
Looking straight ahead, rang his bell
And reached up, beneath a cotton spread...
"Warm and tasty!
There 'aint nuffin like a muffin!"

Next, came the baker with horse-drawn van,
Spreading smells of bread, buns and dung,
Around which children hung to fertilize gardens.
"Come on, horsey...*do* some; *do* some!"
The horse was a gentleman:
Restful, noble, feeding from its nose-bag,
Lashes flickering, tail swishing to keep flies off.

The 'accumulator' man drove a different van,
Supplying acid-filled batteries for radios:
A dangerous load if dropped and damaged;
Somehow we managed.

Saturday was the turn of the 'Corona' man.
Whose bottles were tilted, lest they shifted
When he drove around the corners.
The tops were blocked with marble stops.
Empties were swapped for full ones.
Boys enjoyed the slurping - even more - the burping.

Leather caps with bat-like flaps, aprons, shoulder wraps,
Faces blacked: the most theatrical were the coal men,
Whose leaning sacks - their second backs - were stacked
To hump from lorry to punter's bunker.
Of all the smells we came to know, the freshest was coal,
Even if it *did* take a thousand years to grow.

Overall, we were most in awe
Of an Italian ex-prisoner of war;
His cycle attached to a yellow side-car
Sporting the legend, 'I'm Here!'
Which he couldn't pronounce
So he rang his bell and shouted,
"Ahm Earr! Ahm Earr!"
"Quick, Mum! I'm 'Ere's 'Ere
Gimme' threepence!"

He was a conjuror...not pulling rabbits from hats,
But ice-cream wafers from a shiny, lidded box.
Truly, something to watch!
"Magico!" he would say, flicking his wrist
To place a taste of heaven into a child's eager fist.
"Ahm Earr! Ahm Earr!"

When Rod's first collection of poems, 'Book Ends' was published, he always regretted the fact that there were not enough pages in the book for it to be printed with a spine, so it remained anonymous on a bookshelf. During the last few months of his life, he was working hard to create enough poems to ensure that this collection, 'Putting It Bluntly', would not be 'spineless' (which indeed it isn't, of course!).

Nevertheless, when I felt able at last to prepare 'Putting It Bluntly' for publication, it was deeply disappointing to find that the poems Rod intended for publication still fell short in number to qualify for a spine.

Some fellow poets have written poems inspired by their association with Rod. Mark Skinner, who has undertaken the formatting and layout of the book with such care and patience, suggested that if these poems could be included in an additional section at the end, this would mean that together with line drawings and photographs there would be enough material for the book to have a spine.

I am extremely grateful to Mark for his brainwave, and to the poets who kindly gave permission for their poems to be included. I would also like to say a big thank you to Phil Keen for providing such brilliant line drawing illustrations for two of Rod's poems.

I feel sure Rod would have wholeheartedly approved of our efforts to ensure that 'Putting It Bluntly' is published with a spine. I know he would have been very touched, as I am, by the many different ways in which people have contributed to his book.

Lorraine Bowsher

Dan Haynes

*"Rodney really made you wonder and see what the value
was about doing it. All those years, never giving up, never
being a 'star' but compelled do it, and such a great presence
and never quite sure how serious he was going to be and
you always had to pay such attention or you'd miss
something. I guess he summed up for me the spirit of the
night really."*

Bless this mic
(for Rodney Bowsher)

There isn't such a thing as happiness,
Not in any case how we'd wish there was -
A kind of solid state, a permanence
a bubble that shields us from everything
we do not want, and preserves by some
miraculous means the favourite aspects
of everything we hold dear

There isn't such a thing as happiness.
But there are momentary lapses
from insanity:
there are moments of contact.

There isn't such a thing as everlasting love
a burning homogeneous constancy of flame
that never slips one degree below infinity
never falters, never flickers, never fails.
Love, whatever the hawkers of inadequacy and guilt
may say does choke sometimes on cold mornings,
does stall
on hills

But there is to be sure
a method for ignition
there are such thrusts and roars
and journeys taken together
as road trip movies are made of
moments of contact.

My friends
things are not quite
how we'd want them
we all wish that Rodney was here
when he stood on this stage
he blessed it
and he blessed
this mic too

Bless this mic
and all who take it.
and all who sit before it.
may everyone find
what they came here for.

Bless this mic
it is a chanting pole
a talking post
for oddballs and weirdos
a totem for us roundpegs
to rant about our squareholes
the loves we can't contain
the pains we can't let go of

Bless
this
mic

We wanted fame but we got   acceptance
we wanted a way of life and   we found a place to go
we wanted to change the world   we spoke our minds
we wanted genius   we heard honesty instead
we wanted immortality   and got 4 minutes on this stage.

Somehow
it was more
than we had ever hoped for

Bless this mic.

Ian Beech

"I was delighted when Lorraine asked if she could include this poem in Rodney's new book. I consider it a great honour. Rodney was so well loved in the Devon poetry community, a dear friend who is sadly missed by us all."

Rodney
(after *Nothing Happens Now I'm Old* By Rodney Bowsher)

Nothing's quite the same now you're gone.
I never knew you when you were young
Or during your multifarious careers
But I remember
Meeting you and Lorraine at the Phoenix
And hearing you perform that first time,
A typically hilarious set,
Deadpan delivery,
Taking the Mic for all you were worth.

Nothing's quite the same now you're gone.
But I remember
Shaking your hand, then watching that hand shake,
As you stood and outscored me in the slam,
Your fingers trembling, struggling to separate
The pages that bore your clever words.

Nothing's quite the same now you're gone.
But I remember
Your only visit for lunch
And the dedication you wrote for us
In our copy of *Book Ends*,
A book full of poetic smiles
And poignant reflections
On what was yet to come,
And soon.

Nothing's quite the same now you're gone.
But I remember
The last time I saw you perform,
Increasingly frail,

The prolonged shuffle to the stage
Before proving you'd still got it,
A trooper to the last.
Nothing's quite the same now you're gone.
But I remember
Reading *Hospital*
To your poetry friends,
Your beautifully observed
Description of the place in which you lay.

Nothing's quite the same now you're gone.
But I remember
That last hospital conversation,
Holding your hand
And hearing you say
'Just be yourself.'

Nothing's quite the same now you're gone.
But I remember
Reading your poems to you,
That one last time,
Believing you heard
And your own words brought comfort.

Nothing's quite the same now you're gone.
But I remember
Reading your *Head in the Clouds*
As we mourned you
At the end of your show.

No, nothing's quite the same now you're gone.
But I remember.
We all remember,
Offering Lorraine our love and support.
We remember you
And we remember your words:
So no giving up. And because I tried,
I never died; I never died.

Rodney (after *Nothing Happens Now I'm Old* By Rodney
Bowsher) by Ian Beech, was originally published in Ian's first
collection, 'On the Road to Ollantaytambo',
Poetry Island Press, 2015

Gail Parfitt

*"Rod was always able to be himself. He knew what he
was doing, didn't need to develop a style, but presented his
poetic often acutely humorous verse with an immediate
sense of wisdom and familiarity, coloured by witty insights
and experiences from mid twentieth century culture to the
present day. He was unpretentious, perceptive and
unique, spoke the unsung heroism of ordinary people,
and turned everyday phrases into poetic insight, so they
sometimes became mischievous gems of outspoken genius.
Some of his words are echoed here."*

Not Forgetting Fairness

Rod leans on the pantry door
Post War, (World War Two),
Sees the funny side,
Tongue in cheek.
But looks for something more,
Has a taste for what gets hidden,
Buried, raw.
An appetite for the simple truth
Sandwiched between
The hammed up, pickled side
Of who we are.

Good at lifting the lid
On the stories people tell
But behind net curtains.
Silence rings a bell!
And he takes time to dwell
On what gets stuck
Inside locked doors,
The black comedy of empty drawers,
A murderer's false teeth,
And one slice of beef
Gone missing.

Everyone counts.
And those with airs and graces
Are given funny faces.
Their stuffed shirts ridiculed
With modest aplomb,
While he takes pics of himself
Suited,
With his carpet slippers on.

It was jazz for the asking,
A morning clarinet for cows,
(he really did play to them),
And knowing how the muse mends,
He delighted the crowds.
And even waved a mirror
At 'Music While You Work',
A humming mind filler,
And tea break perk.
But he looked hard at WORK.

How some labour more,
Till God knows when,
Toiling and crawling
All the way to the Crem.
But he didn't reduce
To an 'us' or a 'them',
(Even Vicars with odd socks
Got a look in).
And he was often willing
To lift the hem.

It was said
He had a very busy pen.
And all this, while MPs sat
Firmly on the fence,
Unmoved, or unable
To relent ...
Cash for questions ...
Their defence.

T'was an irreligious account,
Still grounded in ethics and faith,
Suitably laced in the satire
Of a political three legged race.
He even included the injustice
Of the spinning glass divide.
And the Queen's own expendables,
Who appeared more dead than alive.
The soldier's own goal in defence of the realm
Captured by military drill,
While the Ministry of Defence
Makes smarter bombs
For the next theatrical thrill,
Until stilled by peace.

Yes, a vast political cacophany,
Of Industry, Culture and anomie,
With G&T's for the well to do,
And a tea break for me and you ...
While, he got desperately ill.

And quietly, here and there
He puts in a plea for kindness,
To counter his sense of despair.
Reminding us that lives of woe,
Are heartened by love and care,
And that at bottom ...
He wanted to be fair.

He was dead unlucky with his health
And yet he left a wealth of verse.
He's often there with family and friends,
All lodged, as he predicted,
Between book ends.
But maybe,
He's still out there beyond the page,
The old sage,
Playing with happy endings from the inside ...
And every so often, taking the odd bow.

In Homage from
Gail

Lorraine Bowsher

"For Rod"

Laughter Therapy

I envied your clever way with words.
Loved it too, and feared it.
On tenterhooks I'd listen
To jokes told over and over again,
To anyone who crossed your path
Fair game, a captive audience.
No matter if they weren't amused,
You laughed and laughed in the telling,
Longing for others to make you laugh.

But others rarely could in real life.
So you turned instead to the absurd,
The slapstick and perfect timing
Of Norman Wisdom, Tommy Cooper
And of course Dad's Army,
To the sharpshooter repartee
Of U.S. Sergeant Bilko (your favourite),
All this was there - for your enjoyment and mine -
We laughed together, then - and felt the better for it.

Your cleverest (and most subversive) jokes
Were those picked up in the Forces
From the shared banter of a Band of Brothers,
Would be stand up comics,
Nostalgic for NAAFI wartime entertainment
Where many in the laughter business learned their craft.
Released from the irreverent camaraderie
Of your Army service into an indifferent world,
You savoured and honed the taste you'd acquired
For mischief making with the spoken word,
Telling me soldiers call it 'gallows humour'.

The habit persisted throughout your life,
Kept you going through thick and thin.
The humour increasingly acerbic,
No respecter of persons.
You'd return from a solo outing
And tell me who you'd met:
'I nearly said ...', you'd boast.
Your pause was my cue..
'I'm glad you didn't'.
Jokes were what you did.

Was there an opportunity you'd missed?
A fortune to be made
In the world of the Christmas cracker?
Not for a court jester, a Lord of Misrule,
Fuelled by a fierce desire to penetrate
The carapace of convention,
With words that seldom missed their mark.

I found a book you cherished
Of poems, entitled 'Unrespectable Verse'.
All the great poets are represented there
Letting their hair down,
Raging at the status quo
And all the masquerades encountered,
Transforming an innocent into a cynic.
A line you often referred to:
Tennyson's talk of 'the dung of a crow'
Mistaken for a snowdrop.

Timmy Angel Naylor

"I met Rod when, as a young soldier, I joined an Army band in Aldershot, of which he had been a member for several years. We both played clarinet and he quickly took me under his wing and was like a mentor for the two and a half years before he left the Army. I thought him a stylish free spirit.

Rod was an accomplished clarinet player and an energetic tenor saxophone soloist in Dance Band. He introduced me to modern verse, initially through the work of poet and songwriter Rod McKuen. I quickly developed an interest and was soon exploring the world of poetry.

My poem, 'The Man with One Tune' was written about a busker I saw often in Slough who did what it says in the poem. I recognised the honesty of what he did and thought about what he was teaching me. I found him very inspiring."

The Man with One Tune

With a kaftan coat and an Afghan hat
On a box by the side of the road he sat
And played a battered
Piano-accordian.
Time had etched a mystic beauty
Into that weathered Middle Eastern face.
And he had one tune
Just one, just one
As he played in the rain or the morning sun.
I stood, hard listening,
And smugly scanned my
Mental database of music.
And I heard
In that wheezy clatter of notes
The strains of an old Parisian waltz.

Again and again I passed him by
And heard that tune and wondered why.
Some other locals looked askance
At this offbeat man with his tune from France.
But people came to the town for the day,
Saw him there and heard him play
His waltz, and listened once, then, entertained
They carried on.

I wish that I could be like him,
A man without airs.
We enter this world like a bare melody,
As life in a single strand,
But get snagged somehow and woven into
The illusions and delusions of being.
He teaches me
That I could unwind,
Just be that bare melody,
And love life in a single strand
(that each day simply binds two hearts?)

So I loved that man with a tune, just one,
As he played in the rain or the morning sun.
With a kaftan coat and an Afghan hat,
On a box by the side of the road he sat.
I understand a life like that.

Tim King

*"Though traces of Rodney may be gleaned from his
writings, his essence has truly passed. He was both a kind
man and, as evidenced by the title of this book, a blunt
one. When Rodney first came to Taking the Mic he was
already old and frail; yet he delivered his words with
powerful conviction and a mischievous twinkle. Sharp as
a pin. He was an instant hit with young and old alike and
we were honoured to have him perform regularly for us in
the two years leading up to his death. His headline set in
April 2013 was a triumph, though Rodney was way too
modest to ever crow. He had a generosity of spirit, a
respect for others and an implacable inner strength which
stayed with him to the end. He loved and was loved.
Those of us who were lucky enough to know him miss him
greatly."*

Outside the chapel gates
She dips her head
Respectfully

The choice - she thinks - is hers
But Rodney bows her,
Rodney Bowsher

Rodney published his first book of poems, 'Book Ends', in 2014.
A short story and a memoir of his life as a boy soldier can be read
online at www.raddonlines.co.uk
Rodney was a regular Taking the Mic performer at the Phoenix
Arts Centre in Exeter, and contributed poems to the Shobrooke
village newsletter.